The Way We See Things

Middle schoolers look at themselves and issues they face everyday

Iffer Beisswenger
Margaret Eldred

Edited by Carolynne Krusi

Dedications

I would like to dedicate this book to my grandparents, George and Barbara Krusi, because so much of the way I see things is a result of the things that they have given me—Love, wisdom and a world of people whose way of living is so different than mine.

—Iffer Beisswenger

I would like to dedicate this book to Carolynne, because as hard as I have worked on this book, she has worked harder. She has been like a second mother to me my whole life. Carolynne has always been the person who I can talk to, and her house is always a refuge for me.

—Margaret Eldred

The Way We See Things: Middle schoolers look at themselves and issues they face everyday

To order: 603.643.0929

Contents

Editor's Note

By Carolynne Krusi

When Margaret Eldred and Iffer Beisswenger first came to me with the idea of putting together a book of their thoughts about middle school issues, I was ecstatic. Listening in on their thoughtful, humorous and insightful discussions has always been one of my favorite activities, and it was clear that their willingness to address and share their ideas on the difficult challenges of middle school life would be an invaluable gift to others. As a parent of a middle school child, I know there are times when their minds are a mystery. Teachers often wonder who is home inside those adorable heads. Middle school students wonder if they are the only ones out there who feel a certain way. Not only would sharing thoughts in the form of a book be fun, but it might also open doors for others to continue the interesting and sometimes challenging discussions of the issues that Margaret and Iffer address. My role in the project was to be the editor responsible for the logistics of the production of the book. They were very clear that the ideas, revisions, art and decisions were to be theirs. Since they knew more about their own ideas, and I knew more about book making, it seemed to be a great arrangement for all of us.

I assumed that with an advanced degree in Educational Psychology, and several years under my belt as a middle school teacher, guidance counselor, and in curriculum development, I was well versed in the issues of middle school students. As it turns out I have learned more by listening carefully to the hours of discussion that have gone into this book than I did in most of my graduate school classes. Sometimes their words have made me laugh, sometimes they have brought me to tears, and sometimes I have felt awe. The developmental psychologists would say that they are right on track, with one foot in childhood and one in adolescence. I might even have said that myself in my earlier, more analytical years. Now I just say they are treasures. Both are extraordinary human beings, and I feel honored to know them.

Carolynne Krusi is an Assistant Dean at Dartmouth College, Hanover, New Hampshire.

Iffer: I am Iffer (short for Christopher) Beisswenger. I am a thirteen-year-old student in the eighth grade at the Richmond Middle School in Hanover, New Hampshire. I am the youngest in my family with two brothers and one sister. I am a little bit shy which might sound odd for someone who is writing a book, but I have lots of ideas that need to be written. Things that I love are hockey, lacrosse, my friends and my family, and strawberries. I also love spending time at my cabin in the Sierras with no electricity and no phone where I have learned to tell time by the sun on the trees, and I can swim in mountain lakes with my friends. Things I hate include making my bed, basketball, eggnog, and people who are mean to others about things that they can't help.

Margaret: *Things Iffer wouldn't say about himself—Iffer is a wonderful student and an all around nice guy. He is always kind to everyone. Iffer is a really great athlete and always tries his hardest at athletic events. He has been a close friend of mine for as long as I can remember.*

Margaret: I am Margaret Eldred, and I am thirteen years old and live with my family in Hanover New Hampshire, a small New England town. I have three sisters; twin older sisters in high school and a younger sister in fifth grade. I love sports, eating, laughing really loudly, and watching movies with friends. I attend Crossroads Academy, a private school in Lyme, New Hampshire. In the summer I spend time in a cabin on a lake in Canada. There are not a lot of things that I hate, but among them are teacher's pets, people who think they are more cool and much smarter than everyone else, and seeing people in the world who are starving and knowing that there is not enough that I can do to help. I also hate cooked spinach and asparagus.

Iffer: Things that Margaret wouldn't say about herself— She is vivacious and positive and energetic. She's a great student and an awesome athlete. She is kind and positive and has a beauty that comes from the inside out. She's been one of my closest friends since I was six months old, and I feel extremely lucky to know her.

On The Way We Look

Margaret: *Middle school kids worry so much about how they look. In some ways I think it would help to have a uniform so that people would not have to spend time worrying about what to wear. It would be so much easier. Put on your clothes and go to school. Everyone would look the same so there wouldn't be any judgment.*

Iffer: I wouldn't want a uniform. I like to be able to choose my clothes every morning and I think it would get boring to have a uniform. I want to look good, but I don't obsess over it. I don't spend an hour picking my clothes the night before I go to school and that kind of thing.

Margaret: *It think the way they look matters more to girls than it does to boys. People spend a lot of time wondering, "What should I wear? What should I do with my hair?" You want to impress everyone at school. I think that the better looking people are more popular, especially with girls.*

Iffer: I don't understand why girls wear make up. It doesn't really change the way they look. They look good anyway. Why do they wear it?

Margaret: Girls really like it. Before dances girls get together and put on make up and have a great time. No one wears tons of it, but we do like it. It is fun to put on.

Iffer: Seems like a lot of work for not much effect to me.

Margaret: It is interesting to think about who sets the trends regarding what people wear. I think it is mostly the stores. Kids know which stores are cool and what clothes and things are cool within the stores. I am not quite sure how they know this, they just do.

Iffer: Some people at school set the standards for style, too. If one person has a really cool shirt then people will all try to find a shirt like that.

Margaret: It is hard to figure out exactly how people define what is cool. Sometimes it comes from older siblings, sometimes from TV or magazines.

Iffer: Or sometimes it comes from friends, or maybe it is just something that you like.

Margaret: *Hair is a big fashion item, too. For girls now blond and long is cool. Sometimes girls put their hair up, sometimes down, sometimes curly, sometimes not. A lot of people are coloring their hair, too. I think that looks really tacky.*

Iffer: Guys spend a lot of time on their hair as well. They might spend more time on their hair than their clothes. Some guys spend hours spiking their hair and making their hair different colors. I used to spend a lot of time worrying about my hair. Now I just get it wet and put on my hat.

On
Embarassing
Moments

Margaret: I was practicing for the musical, "Oklahoma" in the auditorium on the stage. The practice hadn't really started and we were fooling around on the stage. I started to dance and I did a really high kick. The problem was that I forgot that I had on a tight skirt, so both my legs went right out from underneath me and I landed right on my face.

Iffer: A few years ago I had Jello in my lunch, and I was flirting with this girl. She was really grossed out by Jello, so I was shaking it and wiggling it above her. I was paying more attention to her than the Jello, so I accidentally turned it over and dumped it on her. It is the only thing that I have ever gone to the principal's office for. It wasn't exactly my most romantic move.

Margaret: My dress code says that the shorts that we wear have to be a certain length. The shorts that I wore one day were too short, so one of my teachers was teasing me and tugged on my shorts. They weren't very tight around the waist, so she accidentally pulled my shorts all the way down! Fortunately, I had on a long shirt, but two boys in my class felt they needed to tell everyone in the middle school about it. I was so embarrassed!

on The Internet

Margaret: *The Internet is good for shopping. The place that I live is good for a lot of things, but it has no shopping. It is great to have the Internet to shop.*

Iffer: Hot mail is good, too. IM, Instant Messaging, is good for talking to more than one person at once

Margaret: *IM is good for your typing skills, too, although we use a lot of slang.*

Iffer: IM is great to keep in touch with friends in California and in other far away places. I can talk and find out what is going on with everyone without a long distance bill.

Dictionary of some often used IM terms

ttfn—ta ta for now	Y — why
ttyl—talk to you later	C — see
g2g— got to go	U — you
jk—just kidding	R — are

Iffer: People say different things on IM than in real life because they are not face to face. There is a little more distance so it feels a little safer.

Margaret: *Things can be misinterpreted more easily though because you can't see a person's expression. You don't always know when someone is kidding.*

Iffer: I always feel like I should be careful about anything written because once it is sent, it is out there. It can be kept and held against me or misused or taken out of context. A phone call is sometimes safer.

Margaret: *I don't spend longer than a few minutes a day on IM because it is not entertaining enough to spend long periods of time.*

Iffer: Sometimes I spend longer than others. It depends on how much I have to do, and who I am talking to.

on Homework

Margaret: *There should be homework for every class.*

Iffer: You have to be kidding.

Margaret: *No, I'm not. If you know that you have homework in a class, you will pay closer attention. If you don't have homework you won't pay attention as you go along. When the test comes along you won't remember things as well.*

Iffer: Well, I have to respectfully disagree. It bugs me that we go to school for seven and a half hours, and then we come home and do homework. It seems to me that a creative teacher should be able to teach us the things that they need to teach during the school day.

Margaret: *If you do your homework when you get home from school, there is not much light left when you are finished.*

Iffer: That's part of my point. Most of the students in our area are involved in serious athletics programs outside of school. This is especially important because of the small amount of PE we have in school. Often kids spend two hours in practices or games after school. Many students also have music or religious school as well.

Margaret: *And then there's family time. I like to spend time being with my family and talking to my parents.*

Iffer: That's the problem that I have. There is no time left for either family time or the projects that I want to do on my own. There are things that I like to learn about or explore just because I want to, not because I have to.

Margaret: *I have some things that I'd like to do, too. I can usually fit things in if the homework stays within a reasonable limit.*

Iffer: I'm just glad that no one's thought of giving homework over the summer . . .

Iffer: Groups are really big in middle school. In the public school that I attend the student population is large enough to provide for enough different groups so that there can be a spot for everyone. There are definitely "popular" groups, but also people move between groups a lot, and people are friends with many kinds of people. I sort of resent the portrayal of the popular groups on TV as always shallow, snotty and mean. It's not like that at my school.

Margaret: *At my school, the "popular" group means "pretty" for girls.*

Iffer: In our school the popular group has been friends a long time. They are likely to make out with their girl-friends or boyfriends and do things like that. It's not that they are necessarily more apt to have boyfriends or girl-friends, it's more what they do with them.

Margaret: *At the private school I attend, there are sometimes people left out because there are so few people. If a group of people does anything, it is possible that others might feel left out. And there is definitely a group that is more socially oriented and a group whose interests are in other areas.*

Iffer: The problem with groups in general, and especially the importance put on the popular group, is that people sometimes feel so hurt if they are not included. People sometimes even try to be what they feel other people want them to be instead of who they really are so people will like them and include them. But if people like you for who you're not, what's the point? Isn't it more fun to hang out with the not-so-popular kids you like?

Margaret: *Yeah, really.*

on Teachers

Margaret: *A good teacher asks a lot of questions and makes you think.*

Iffer: Good teachers are fun and funny. They keep class entertaining and make you laugh. They interact with students, but don't let kids take advantage of them. Also, when teachers add games to hard work, it makes the work more fun. Games are also a fun way to firm up the ideas that we learn in class. My math teacher does a great job of rewarding us with games after tough classes and it really livens things up.

Margaret: *A good teacher asks questions so kids have to be alert. If he or she just lectures all the time, then kids know they don't have to pay attention.*

Iffer: If a teacher must give homework, then it should be a reasonable amount. It should pertain to the work in class and be challenging, not boring. Homework should never be a waste of the students' time.

Margaret: *A teacher should use words that students understand. I hate it when teachers use a higher-level vocabulary and leave everyone in the dust, or talk down to us like we are little kids.*

Iffer: A good teacher makes you feel comfortable and at home in class. My English teacher has set up a class that is really welcoming. It makes me want to contribute to discussions and participate in class.

Margaret: *Good teachers show students that they care about them in many ways, not just in their school lives but in their whole lives. When a student knows that a teacher really cares, it makes a student want to try harder in a class.*

Iffer: A good teacher is careful to be sure that boys and girls are treated equally both in class and out of class. Boys and girls should be called on equally, treated similarly for the same disciplinary infractions and have the same expectations set for them. It is almost never the way it happens, and only a few teachers seem to notice. There have been so many times that the boys and girls do exactly the same thing in the lunchroom in elementary school, for instance, and the boys have been sent out of the room, and the girls have been asked nicely not to do it again. A few years ago there were several boys and one girl in my class who misused a piece of playground equipment. The school punished the group by denying the whole class of boys the use of the equipment, even those who were not involved in the incident at all. The girls, even the one who was involved, could continue to use the equipment if they wanted. Good teachers should stand up for kids and not let that kind of unfair discipline happen. It's like they believe the rhyme about girls being "sugar and spice and everything nice," and boys being "snakes and snails and puppy dog tails." They seem to look for it and expect it in our behavior

Margaret: *Some of the teachers really do treat the boys unfairly. Some definitely do have "teacher's pets" that they like better than everyone else, so they treat them differently than the other kids.*

Iffer: A good teacher is someone a student would go to if he or she had a problem or a concern in or out of school. Teachers in middle school can be really important people in students' lives.

on Peer Pressure

Iffer: Peer pressure is pretty strong in middle school. There are things all around us that are new for a lot of us, so there are times when most of us don't feel all that secure. When people are insecure, they think they have to do what everyone else does to fit in. I think when we feel more secure in ourselves and with our friends, we are more comfortable being individuals. We can do things that are just what we want, which may or may not be different than the group. I know that's how I feel.

Margaret: *Sometimes people justify going along with peer pressure by assuming that it doesn't really count because what they are doing is just for one night. Or they think that if a bunch of other people are doing it, it must be okay. Everyone assumes that if something were a really bad idea, someone else would say no or stop things, so they don't have to.*

Iffer: There are a bunch of insecure people out there so it might not be a good assumption that someone else is more likely to do something sensible than you. There are a lot of people who are looking to other people to set the stage for them. That goes for a lot of things, from clothes, to sports, to things to do at a party.

Margaret: *There's not much you can do about the fact that we will all face peer pressure, and it is a lot easier if you know it and can identify it. Then, at least, you feel you have a choice when it comes up.*

Iffer: At this age when you are with older kids, you feel like there is an expectation that you should "live a little" and "not be a weenie."

Margaret: *Everyone is trying to impress each other, but really often it ends up that no one has much fun doing it. It is so much more relaxing to feel like you can really be yourself. Friends are sometimes a help and are sometimes part of the problem. If they are sucked in to trying to impress other people they are likely to put pressure on you to join them, and you don't feel like you have any support to be yourself. Also, you usually trust your friends' judgement, so you are more likely to figure that if your friend is doing something, it is probably a good idea. That trust only works if your friend is making a good decision.*

Iffer: Mostly, if you have the right kind of friends, they are supportive of you as an individual, whether or not you do the same things that they are doing. You feel free to be yourself with really good friends.

Margaret: *The better you feel about yourself, the less likely you are to be influenced by peer pressure.*

on **The Environment**

Margaret: *I think our generation worries a lot about the environment and what will happen to it as we grow up.*

Iffer: Things like the rain forest and the hole in the ozone layer are problems that seem out of our control, but will have a big impact on all of us in the future.

Margaret: *It is hard to deal with the big things so we try to deal with the smaller things that we can have some control over, like recycling and picking up trash.*

Iffer: I think it would be exciting to be involved in some larger-scale, alternative transportation projects, like golf carts for in-town use. How cool would that be?

Margaret: *Yes! We don't need huge cars for getting around town. We could use solar powered golf carts. And give drivers' licenses to thirteen year olds!*

on Pets

Margaret: *I love my dogs. I think everyone should have pets. They are so cute. Cats are fun, too, but they sort of do whatever they want. They play with you more when they are kittens. The dogs are always happy to see you. Cats are happy to see you when they are hungry.*

Iffer: There are days when everything seems to go wrong, and I am frustrated and in a bad mood. Then I come home and see my dog, Puck, and I can't help but feel better.

Margaret: *It is so hard to get mad at them when they do something wrong and they look at you with that cute look on their face. They look up at you with those big eyes, and you just want to say, "Oh well, don't do it again."*

Iffer: I think pets are really good for teaching responsibility. Kids have to think about another living thing and its needs; feeding it, giving it water, grooming it, exercising it or whatever the needs of the pet are.

Margaret: *And going for walks can get everyone out for exercise. Sometimes it gives us a chance to go out as a family.*

Iffer: Sometimes I have to admit, walking the dog before school on cold mornings is not my favorite thing. Even if she is cute.

Margaret: *Pets are really good company when you are lonely. It is nice to have someone to cuddle with when you are watching TV or when you are reading.*

Iffer: And if you have done everything wrong and everyone is mad at you, and it is a bad hair day, you always know that your dog loves you no matter what. It can't help but make you smile.

41

on Bodies. Changing

Iffer: I really don't think that we need to talk about bodies changing.

Margaret: Actually, I think it's really important. I think it's on a lot of kids' minds. When we were in 6th grade, if you were developing faster than everyone else was, you probably felt self-conscious or uncomfortable. Sometimes people even made fun of people about wearing bras, or being tall, or starting to get moustache hairs early or things like that.

Iffer: Okay, so bodies change. People grow up. Big deal. Now, let's change the subject.

Margaret: Then, by 8th grade, people have started to feel uncomfortable if they *haven't* started developing yet. We all go to the beach and half the people are checking each other's bathing suits. It is really tough if you are not changing at exactly the same time as everyone else. It's hard to be the tallest girl or the shortest boy. I know guys who have a really hard time in sports or at dances because they haven't had their growth spurts yet.

Iffer: And I know guys who are really uncomfortable talking about this kind of stuff . . .

Margaret: *Hey, you wouldn't be the hockey player you are now if you still had your sixth grade body.*

Iffer: Hockey, now there's a good subject, let's talk about that.

Margaret: *The reason to talk about things that make you uncomfortable is to understand that you aren't the only one who feels that way. If middle school kids knew that other people felt the same way, or at least understood, it might make things better.*

Iffer: Okay. You win. Are we done talking about this yet?

Margaret: *Well we haven't even started talking about zits.*

Iffer: Oh, please. I think I hear my mother calling . . .

on Dating

Margaret: *Dating is an interesting issue because in 6th grade, people "go out" mostly just to "go out." You don't actually go anywhere. It is just to identify that you like a certain guy and he likes you. I think kids do it to have a little romance in their lives. It gives everyone something to talk about.*

Iffer: An average 6th grader just goes out to go out. Maybe they've kissed but usually not much more than that. A relationship could last one or two days, or could last two months.

Margaret: *It wouldn't be a big deal if you didn't have a boyfriend, because you could talk about everyone else's.*

Iffer: I might be a little sad if I didn't have a girlfriend in 6th grade, but I'd get over it. By 7th grade I might start to feel differently. I might start feeling a little badly about myself if no girls liked me at all.

Margaret: *Our school is different. Our class is so small, and we have all been together for so long that we are all like brothers and sisters. I can't imagine going out with anyone at my school.*

But some people do go out with people outside of the school. In terms of what people do, I think our actions probably match those of our friends in the public school pretty well. I remember a couple of years ago there was a big issue with the teachers about people dancing too close at a dance. I think someone might even have been kissed. That's a big deal at our school dances.

Iffer: Some romances go beyond kissing in 7th grade, but not many. Do you think you will be going out on dates in 8th grade?

Margaret: Yes, I plan to go out to the movies and places like that.

Iffer: Me, too. I have a question for you. Who do you think should pay for things on dates?

Margaret: I assume we would split things half and half. But, if I were a guy, I think I would bring enough money to pay for both just in case.

Iffer: That's a good idea, but I think I would be mad if a girl just expected me to pay for her. And what about the "rules"? How do you communicate what you feel comfortable doing and not doing in terms of touching?

Margaret: *If someone wanted to do something I didn't want to do, I'd just point to the movie screen and say, "Oh, look! This is a really interesting part of the movie!" or, "Maybe it's time for a walk!"*

Iffer: I think I might just say, "I'm not ready for that right now." It is hard to be clear about what you want without hurting someone's feelings, but I think you'd feel worse if you did things you didn't feel good about.

on Sports

Margaret: *Sports are so important to keep me in shape. I would not be as happy if I didn't play a sport.*

Iffer: Sometimes when I feel restless or bored in school, I think forward to the afternoon and realize that I have a practice or a game coming up. It makes the day go faster if I have something to look forward to.

Margaret: *It is really nice to have a break between school and homework. I can think much more clearly once I have had some exercise and some time to be with my friends.*

Iffer: There are a lot of things that we learn through sports. Teamwork is probably the most important. In most sports the success of the team has less to do with the talent of any single person than the ability of the whole group to work together. It always feels so great when the team really works together well.

Margaret: *I work equally hard for both school and sports.*

Iffer: I also really like the fact that athletics offer me the chance to meet people that I might not have gotten to know otherwise. After a season of hockey our team becomes really close because we spend so much time together and work so hard together. We really have fun together.

Margaret: *I think that I am more organized when I have a sport because I have to be more careful about my time when I have a practice or a game. I am more careful to get my homework done early.*

Iffer: I'll do my homework the night before a long practice or a game during the week or on Thursday if there is a tournament on the weekend. I need to get more organized for the weekend if I have games scheduled. I think sports are helpful for time management, especially when I have two sports overlapping, like soccer and hockey do in the fall. There are nights when I can have three hours of practice or games, and if I combine that with two hours or more of homework, plus dinner, there's not much time left to breathe. If I don't manage my time well, I regret it very soon.

Margaret: *Sports are also a great way to see friends. Especially going to a private school, I like having a chance to get together with friends from other places.*

Advice we've Heard Too Much

Iffer: There are a few pieces of advice that every middle school student has heard a thousand or more times. Someone should realize that after a while it stops being useful to say the same thing over and over. Any middle school student who hasn't figured out that smoking causes cancer by now is really asleep at the switch.

Margaret: *"Don't drink," and, "Don't do drugs," are on that list. And then there is always the advice that, "Too many sweets are bad for you." We've heard that a few times as well.*

Iffer: "Why can't you be more like your brother or sister?" is advice from parents that is not only useless, but guaranteed to infuriate any middle school kid.

Margaret: *"Get a good education. Go to college!" We get it; we get it. We promise.*

on 'Advice We Need

Iffer: There are some issues that we really do need help with. For instance, what in the world are we supposed to do about the six-billion-dollar national debt that we are being left with? It is very frightening.

Margaret: *It would be nice to know how people find jobs that they really like so they really enjoy their days at work.*

Iffer: When you watch movies you see a couple kissing, then the next thing you know, they are in bed. We have heard all of this discussion about "safe sex" and "consensual sex" but where are the examples of the real-people conversations that we are supposed to have in order to get there? We never see anyone in the movies or anywhere else having those tough conversations. These aren't exactly part of our everyday conversations, and it is not like people would just automatically *know* how to have conversations like this. It would be nice to have some advice.

Margaret: *Who do grownups go to for help when they don't have parents or teachers anymore?*

Iffer: We see our friends whose parents have been through divorces, and we realize how difficult things can be. Maybe it would be helpful to have a class in things we should know about relationships. It might be more useful than the quadratic equation (although my mom insists that the quadratic equation will be useful someday for something).

Margaret: *And I have a question. Why do kids smoke even though we all know that it causes cancer and it tastes bad? We don't think it's cool now, but somehow by the end of high school many kids are already addicted. What's the deal with that?*

Iffer: Along a different line, how do you know what to do when someone you really care about is making a decision that you really think is a mistake for them, and you don't want to betray the trust of your friend?

on
Parents

Margaret: *What makes a good parent is when I have a fight with one of my sisters, they should listen to both sides of the argument and pay attention to what both sides have to say before they decide who is right and wrong, and who should be punished.*

Iffer: Parents should be involved in kids lives and strict enough to know what you are doing, but not so strict that they keep you from going out at all.

Margaret: *Parents should give kids freedom. But it should not be too much freedom so that kids can't get into too much trouble.*

Iffer: And kids should be able to increase their privileges by acting responsibly.

Margaret: *Good parents look at what you are doing and what you are wearing and what you are eating. They shouldn't let you eat only junk food or wear inappropriate clothing.*

Iffer: I agree.

Margaret: On the other hand, parents have to remember that the fashions have changed since they were kids and they should not expect us to wear what they wore.

Iffer: Yes, for instance, just because a pair of pants is made of flannel it doesn't mean they are pajamas. And long hair does not make you a bad student.

Margaret: Tucking in shirts is not cool anymore. It is fine to have a little stomach showing, but not too much.

Iffer: The most important things that parents can do for their kids are to love them and to listen to them. Really listen with their whole heart. I know that I have parents who love me. Not all kids are as lucky.

Margaret: I know what you mean. I feel lucky, too.

Iffer: Last summer when I was traveling I was in a situation that really made me uncomfortable. I was with a friend who realized that he was going to miss a deadline to meet his mother. I watched his reaction and it was obvious that he was terribly frightened about what would happen to him. My parents would have been mad if I missed a deadline too, but this fear was a different kind of fear than I have ever felt about a punishment. It was a fear that kids shouldn't have to feel. It was clear that something very bad was going to happen to him for being late. He wouldn't let me walk back with him, but I could see the tears well up in his eyes as he walked away from me.

   After thinking about it for a long time, I decided to talk to my mom about it. I really felt that something was wrong. If he was being hurt, it was important that someone knew about it. I knew that my mom would know how to talk to someone in a way that made sure that he would be safe. She spoke with someone who was trained to help with the assurance of confidentiality.

on Music & Art

Margaret: *I really enjoy art. I like making art and I enjoy seeing art. My favorite is modern art when I am not trying to copy anything.*

Iffer: If I really try hard then I can make a decent excuse for a picture, but usually I am just hopeless. But I do appreciate art itself and it is really important to me.

Margaret: *My favorite art is collage. I really enjoy making collages out of newspaper and magazine clippings.*

Iffer: How about art museums? I like them once in a while. Unfortunately my parents have a higher tolerance for museums than I do.

Margaret: *Whenever we travel the main priority for my mother is cultural education and art museums. That's okay, but two museums a day is <u>too</u> much! It makes you need exercise!*

Iffer: I love listening to music and watching people play. I like to imagine myself playing, but I know it is a dream. I think that I am musically challenged. I don't have enough time to play much other than the CD player right now. Maybe at some other phase of my life I will be able to learn an instrument.

Margaret: *I played the piano for a long time because my mom made me. I don't think parents should force middle school kids to play an instrument if they don't want to. But I do love listening to music.*

Iffer: Me, too. I can't listen to it while I study, though, I find it too distracting. I get sidetracked into a play mood not a work mood.

Margaret: *I love to listen to music when I study. It relaxes me and helps me to focus. One thing is true though about teen-age music today, you should never take the words to songs seriously. They are almost all ridiculously stupid. If you follow the advice in some of the songs, you will get yourself in serious trouble, or seriously confused.*

what's

young

cool

now

cool

why not,

RADIANT GLOW,

We Were Not Told to Lie

ice cream

diva

boys

Great Hair

trim down and tone up

summer soul.

shop

CASH

splash

on
God &
Religion

Margaret: *Do you believe in God?*

Iffer: Yes, but I am not sure about organized religion or church.

Margaret: *I believe in God, too, but I have some questions.*

Iffer: My sense is that God really wants us to be kind and thoughtful and take good care of other people.

Margaret: *I think it is really more about trying to practice the virtues like kindness, and patience and tolerance of others than going to a lot of religious events. I think being nice and kind is more important than going to church every Sunday.*

Iffer: I have a hard time believing that God wanted all of those nations of people to kill each other over religion. If God represents peace, it is hard to understand how people feel that it is right to have wars in the name of religion.

Margaret: It is not that either the Bible or the Koran says that people should kill each other. But it is people who interpret the messages and sometimes they have reasons to use it as an excuse to make war.

Iffer: That is a good point.

on Privileges

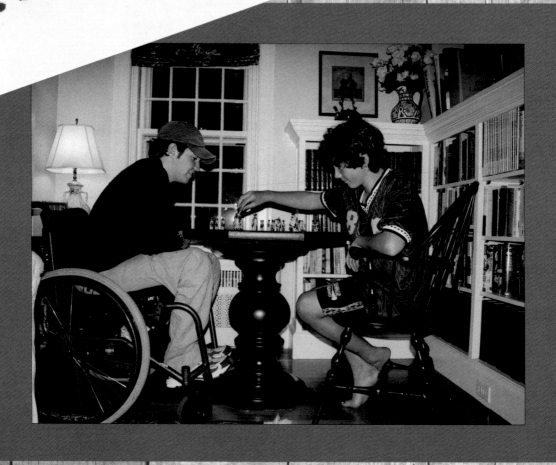

Margaret: *At school we get a lot of freedom because we are the eighth graders. We get to make a lot of decisions and people look up to us. We are responsible for dances and decisions about events that happen at school.*

Iffer: In our school eighth graders get out for lunch early. That doesn't seem like a big deal, but there is a long lunch line, so if you get there first, you don't have to use your whole lunch period in line. Getting to the lunch line first is a huge privilege for people in our school.

Margaret: *I don't have specific privileges that I work for at home, but if I do well in school, and I'm generally responsible, then I earn more respect from my parents. After that they are likely to give me more privileges.*

Iffer: If I prove myself to my parents by being responsible when I go out, like coming home on time, being where I say I'm going to be, and making good decisions, then I can talk them into more privileges the next time I go out, like staying out later.

Margaret: *Yes, I have found that works, too.*

Iffer: There are other kinds of privileges, too. Some of them you are not even aware of until they go away or until someone else points them out. My brother-in-law was in a car accident with my sister last Christmas, and he is now a quadriplegic. It has changed the way I see things so much. Now, I wake up in the morning and realize that being able to walk is a privilege that not all people have. Not everyone can get into restaurants and stores by walking in the front doors. Some people can't even walk down the street without people looking at them with odd looks. Some privileges you take for granted until you realize how difficult it is for someone who doesn't have them.

Margaret: *My step grandmother had a stroke that has made it hard for her to move her arm and hand. She is a composer and she plays the piano and organ. She can't do what she really, really loves. It would be really hard not to be able to do what you love. She is such a wonderful person. She seems to be happy anyway, and everyone loves her so much.*

Iffer: The same with my brother-in-law. He has a

million friends. And he's an athlete and incredibly determined to learn how to do amazing things on his own. Speaking of privileges, it is a real privilege to know him, and an inspiration. I am finding out that there are some other kinds of privileges, too.

Margaret: *Some of the issues of privilege have to do with the area we live in. When you are a white person in an area that is mostly white, you have the privilege of having people treat you as an individual, and assume that you have your own ideas and thoughts about things. If you happen to be from the Middle East, all of a sudden people treat you like you are a terrorist just because of how you look.*

Iffer: And if you are white in our town you have the privilege of buying Band-Aids that match your skin color, or having your hair cut by someone who knows how to cut your kind of hair. These are things that are simple in my life because I have the privilege of not having to worry about them. It makes me sad that it is not as true for some of my non-white friends. Privileges don't always seem to be handed out fairly.

on Money

Margaret: *Money is good. You can buy clothes with it.*

Iffer: I like money a lot too. But there are some things about money that worry me. I worry about how to support myself. I worry about how our country can support itself. I worry a lot about the things we have learned in Social Studies, that so much of the world's resources rest in the hands of so few people. In some ways it would be helpful if there could be a system that might make it so that everyone would have enough money to get by. I guess the Communists tried that, and it didn't seem to work very well.

Margaret: *It really wouldn't be fair to have a system where people that have made the effort to get more education and become more trained would get the same pay as those who have done nothing.*

Iffer: And if those who worked harder would be rewarded the same way as the people who didn't do much at all, why would people want to work harder?

Margaret: *On the subject of our own money, I think that parents should let kids budget their own money. Obviously we can budget the money that we earn ourselves, but we can't earn all the money that we need for all our clothes and stuff yet. My parents put money in an account every six months for me, and I am responsible for buying all of my own clothes and things that I need. It has really helped me learn to budget and save. If my money is used up before the end of my six months, then I have to give up buying things.*

Iffer: I really like money, I just don't like the part where I have to work for it. I really like the money tree concept, or maybe we could get one of those geese that lays the golden eggs.

Margaret: *I like food. I like all kinds of food. I especially like chocolate croissants and smoothies. Smoothies are so good; they are the best ever! Yum!*

Iffer: I like food, too. I mostly eat when I come home from school at the end of the day, because I am always so hungry then. In order to save money, I don't buy very much at school. Food is expensive at school, and it is so bad for you. It is pretty greasy and high calorie food.

Margaret: *I really like salad with good dressing. I don't pay too much attention to eating healthy food, but the foods that I crave are generally healthy ones.*

Iffer: I pay some attention to trying to eat healthy food. I don't eat forty brownies at a time. I'll eat only ten or so instead.

Margaret: I don't usually crave unhealthy stuff. The other day I was dying for some bread with goat cheese. I don't know how healthy that is but it was sooo good!

Iffer: I really like to eat cereal. My brother and I go through tons of cereal when he is home.

Margaret: If I had a friend who was overweight, I think I would ask that friend to exercise with me.

Iffer: I get very angry when I see overweight people being teased. It makes me mad when people are not recognized for who they are inside. Weight is a big issue with our age group, both the girls and the boys.

Margaret: If I had any friends that I worry might be getting too thin, I would offer food and encourage them to eat it, "These are really good; try one!" If they got serious, then I'd get serious, too. If not, I would try to bring up the subject by joking about eating, "Trust me, these are really good!"

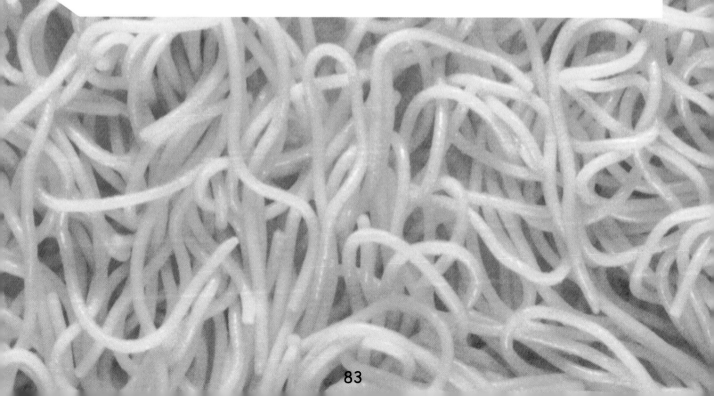

Iffer: Eating disorders are really serious and can kill people. You really need to tell someone, a parent or a teacher or a counselor. If your friends find out, they might get mad, but one day they are going to thank you. If it is a good friend, and he or she doesn't realize that you are helping, hopefully that will become clear soon enough. As you know, there are friends of ours that are having a hard time with eating disorders, so it is important that we understand them as much as we can.

on Following rules

Iffer: How do you decide which rules are okay to break and which ones you shouldn't break?

Margaret: *That's a good question. When I was younger I had a hard time with the dress code rules at school. I wanted to break them. But now I see things a little differently. I see school more as my job. I think that there are appropriate clothes to wear for your "job" that aren't necessarily the same as the clothes you wear to hang out in. It is easier to follow rules if the rules make sense to you.*

Iffer: Sometimes there are completely ridiculous rules, like the sign that says, "No Standing." What do they want you to do, fly?

Margaret: *Parents usually think about rules before they make them. Even if we don't like the rules there are usually important reasons for them so it's a good idea to follow them. But the parents have to make the rules understandable so we don't think the rules are stupid and want to rebel.*

Iffer: What about rules like the orders that were given to soldiers in Nazi Germany? What about the people who followed rules there? There are times when you should not follow rules if the rules are unethical.

Margaret: *If there are rules that don't fit in with what you believe, then you may have to break them. There may be consequences, though. I guess you have to be ready for that.*

Iffer: What about clubs with rules like drinking a keg of beer? Rules don't just come from parents or the government. They can come from other places as well. There might be medical reasons for not following rules as well as ethical ones.

Margaret: *You're right. And another thing that is important when you are going to break a rule is having a really good understanding of the whole situation. Knowledge of what is happening and the possible consequences before making a decision to break a rule, is really important, otherwise you can get yourself* or other people in a lot of trouble. On the other hand, there are times you could get yourself or others into more trouble by not breaking a rule.

Iffer: Sometimes life is so complicated.

on Friendship

Iffer: Friends are a really, really important part of middle school.

Margaret: *A good friend is someone who you can trust not to tell your secrets. In middle school that kind of trust is really hard to find. Everyone tells everyone else everyone's secrets. It's awful.*

Iffer: I agree. Trust is really important.

Margaret: *There are some other things that are important in friendships besides trust. A friend is also someone who is fun to be around, polite, and nice not only to the kids everyone likes, but to the not-cool kids as well; someone who is nice to everyone.*

Iffer: A good friend would go out of his way to help you out. It is someone you would call on to help you if you need it. Someone you would ask for advice, or help with homework or things like that. Also, a friend is someone you would call if you wanted to do something fun, go hiking or out to pizza or whatever.

Margaret:. *A good friend is someone who would tell you that you were being mean if you were being mean.*

Iffer: It is unusual to have a really close friend of the opposite sex. Margaret and I are really lucky to have each other. We have known each other all of our lives so we can be really honest with each other. There are a lot of times we can help each other out, like when she needs more guys at her dances. Sometimes we need help figuring out what girlfriends or boyfriends might be thinking, so we ask each other.

Margaret: *A good friend will also be there for you when things go badly. If you don't make the team you are hoping to make, for instance, it is nice to have a friend who understands.*

Iffer: Sometimes when a really close friend of yours goes through a difficult time, you feel like you go through it with them. Middle school is a tough time for a lot of kids. Some of my best friends have struggled with some issues that have been hard for them, and it almost makes me wish I could go through the difficult times for them. It makes me realize how much my friends are a part of me, and how much I miss them and care about them when we can't be together. Good friends are some of the most valuable things in life.

on Video Games

Margaret: *I don't understand video games. How can you play them for hours?*

Iffer: I really do like them. And I don't do them for hours, but they are good for relaxation. They're fun. They develop great thumb muscle skills. And car driver skills!

Margaret: *You're joking right?*

Iffer: No, of course not.

Margaret: *Real driving is so different.*

Iffer: You mean you can't run into the little old ladies and cows in real life?

Margaret: *And when the police follow you, you don't ever have to pull over?*

Iffer: And while you are being responsible and grown up, aren't you going to yell at me about the violence of shooting random aliens out of the sky on the television screen?

Margaret: *I do think kids playing violent games for hours enhances violence in our society.*

Iffer: I have never left a video game and had any desire to hurt anyone. I can see your point though. There is a difference between Mario shooting water guns and some of the games with huge macho guys on steroids with oozies blowing up everything in sight. A steady diet of violent TV and violent video games probably is not good for children and other living things. It doesn't exactly develop the same kind of creative approach to life that climbing mountains and getting together with friends might offer.

Margaret: *But I have to admit some of the games are sort of fun.*

Iffer: Okay, let's go play one quickly before you are overcome by another fit of maturity.

Thank You

- to our parents and grandparents for their encouragement and support, for ignoring the messes that we made, and for not getting mad when we were late for dinner.

- to Adam, Ben, Rebecca, Owen, Virginia, Elizabeth and Annie for their ideas, help and enthusiasm, and for not minding when we got more than our share of attention.

- to Kate for her helpful input into the conversations and to Nick for his patience and sense of humor.

- to Beth for knowing about books and Jean for knowing about middle school students

- to Lynne McRae, Meg Gallagher, Carl Lovejoy, Tom and Anne Gamble and Kristin Barlup for reviewing our book for us.

- to Susan Finer and the Richmond School teachers and Jean Behnke and the Crossroads teachers for teaching us and believing in us.

- to John LaCrosse for giving us the chance to share our book with others.

- to Barbara Jones for her vast technical knowledge and help.